BE-LOVED

*A five-week journey into deeper intimacy
with the Lover of our souls*

Cindy Powell

Cover art by Aeron Brown: www.aeronbrown.com

Published by Simple Faith Press: P.O. Box 1614, Redlands, CA 92373

All Scripture quotations, unless otherwise indicated, are taken from the Holy Bible, New International Version®, NIV®. Copyright © 1973, 1978, 1984, 2011 by Biblica, Inc.™ Used by permission of Zondervan. All rights reserved worldwide. www.zondervan.com The "NIV" and "New International Version" are trademarks registered in the United States Patent and Trademark Office by Biblica, Inc.™ Copyright © 1973, 1978, 1984 by International Bible Society. Used by permission of Zondervan Publishing House.

ISBN-10: 1975689011

ISBN-13: 78-1975689018

CONTENTS

OTHER BOOKS BY THE AUTHOR

The Key to His Heart: Unlocking God's heart for one church, one body, and one bride. A devotional exploration of Jesus' prayer in John 17.

Love Letters: From His Heart to Yours. Thirty days of devotional encouragement.

HR Matters: What you don't know can hurt your ministry. An essential book on human resources specific to churches and ministries.

All the above are currently available on amazon.com. For more information, visit: www.cindypowell.org

COMING SOON

Twelve Timeless Tales of Truth: Modern spiritual allegories that reveal timeless truths.

Spontaneous Devotions: A collaborative collection of spontaneous expressions of worship and encouragement. Compiled with artist Aeron Brown.

Journal of a Misunderstood Mystic: A compilation of devotional ponderings, biblical meditations, and other musings designed to encourage Jesus-loving contemplatives and creatives who may have found it difficult to thrive within the tightly structured paradigms that define much of the modern church.

Introduction

I really only have one message in life: *Jesus loves you.*

Familiar words. We know them in theory. Maybe we've even tasted the truth of these simple but powerful words. But do we really *believe* them? Do we really *know* how much He loves us? Do we know it in our knowers—within the deepest core of our being? Do our lives demonstrate the security and confidence of those who *know* they are loved and cherished by the One whose opinion matters above all? I can't say that is what I have personally observed and experienced within the Church.

Years ago, I was having coffee with a friend and she remarked, "We need to move people away from this self-focus on how much God loves them personally and get them thinking about how much He loves *other* people. It's not about us!" She was sincere. There was a lot of truth to what she was sharing. But there was one small problem: When you "move people on" before they truly *know* Love—before they know love that passes knowledge and love that drives out fear—their foundation will *never* be secure.

The Church has done a great job of teaching the *theology* of God's love, but we've done a lousy job of actually connecting people to His heart. Even more, we've done a lousy job of modeling His love—to each other *and* to the world around us.

There *is* a lot of self-focus in the Church, but I can pretty much guarantee it's *not* because we're too focused on how much God loves us personally. Self-focus is never the fruit of love—it's the fruit of fear. It's the fruit of orphan-spirited beggars running around "trying" to love other orphan-spirited beggars, because we know that's what we're supposed to be doing.

It hasn't worked out very well.

Maybe we need to back up a few steps. Maybe we need to lay down our lofty theology and pseudo maturity, and take a little breather in His presence. Maybe we need to get gut wrenchingly honest about how much of His love is really filling our lives. Maybe we need to take some time to focus, really focus, on the Source of love. Maybe we need to take the time to press in to hear what *He* thinks about us.

Maybe we need to step back and simply allow ourselves to *be-loved*.

That is the whole point of the next five weeks. My hope and prayer is that the simple but profound message—that Jesus loves *you*—will take on new life. I hope and pray that your heart will be captured afresh, that your mind will be renewed in truth, and that you will rest in the astounding reality that now, always, and forever...

You are His beloved!

Week 1
Laying the Foundation:
"Learning to Be-Loved"

Intimacy. What is it? More specifically, what does it mean in our relationship with Jesus? Is it something to be desired? The dictionary defines intimacy as: *close familiarity or friendship; closeness.* One catchy definition I've often heard is "in-to-me-see." Intimacy is a place of vulnerability and authenticity. It's a place where there are no pretenses; a place where you know and are fully known—without shame. In a very real sense, intimacy with God is a return to the freedom and innocence of the Garden of Eden where Adam and Eve were "naked and unashamed."

Sadly, we're a long way from the freedom and innocence of Eden. Our senses are continually assaulted by a million and one distractions luring us away from the beauty and simplicity of intimate fellowship with our Creator—the very thing we were created to know.

Yet His desire has never changed. He still yearns for intimate communion with His children. He still longs to walk with us in the cool of the day. Although He already knows everything about us, He wants us to *invite* Him into the deepest places of our hearts—just as He wants to share His own.

> *"But now you have been united with Christ Jesus. Once you were far away from God, but now you have been brought near to him through the blood of Christ."*
>
> **– Ephesians 2:13 NLT**

Intimacy is the journey of drawing ever closer to God's heart. We are His beloved and He wants us to be-loved! It is the process coming to know and love Him more fully and allowing Him to know and lavish His love more fully upon us. He already knows us inside and out (and still loves us!) but He wants the present tense *experience* of our companionship, just as He wants us to experience His. Since intimacy is something you experience, it can't be merely taught or imparted. Intimacy is the result of an ever deepening *relationship* and not simply a subject to be learned. **It is something you personally develop with God over time**.

If intimacy is something experienced and developed out of relationship, why create a study for this purpose? Although there is no teaching, no prayer, no five-step formula, and no program that can *ever* lead you into intimacy with God, I believe there *is* a place for teaching in the process.

The objective of this five-week journey is three-fold:

1. To dismantle some of the wrong theological ideas that can keep us from truly knowing God's heart.

2. To stir a deeper hunger in our hearts to *want* to know God more intimately.

3. To provide a few simple examples, tools and hands-on activities to help jumpstart and/or deepen our individual journeys into intimacy.

As a framework for our discussion, we'll examine intimacy with God first through the death, burial, and resurrection of Christ, and we'll end with our call to action in the Great Commission. Each of these unique stages of Jesus' ministry and mission to restore our intimate connection with God contain precious keys that can be used to unlock a greater depth of communion with Him.

Aside from this introductory lesson, which is a bit shorter and differs in format, each lesson will include three sections:

1. **Study** ~ A brief look at a story or two from Scripture relevant to the lesson's main subject matter, along with a few relevant questions for digging deeper.

2. **Stir** ~ Personal testimony and application that puts the lesson into action with the goal of stirring hunger and expectation within your own heart. As in the "Study" section, there will be a few relevant questions at the end of the section to help apply the information.

3. **Start** ~ Simple tools and activations to help you get started in your desire to go deeper. Since we're all wired differently, you may find some of these more helpful and relevant to you than others. Focus on those that are the most meaningful to you.

If you are doing the study on your own, you may find it helpful to take a different day of the week to focus on each section.

My journey. To start off, I thought it would be helpful to share a bit of my own journey, including what prompted me to develop this "Be-Loved" series. It all started with a question:

What does faithfulness look like in this season?

> *"To fall in love with God is the greatest of all romances; to seek Him, the greatest adventure; to find Him, the greatest human achievement. "*
>
> **–Augustine**

As is frequently the case, I was surprised by the Lord's answer. Before I share that, let me share a bit more about myself. I tend to be one of those "highly sensitive" types. In fact, I've been accused of being *overly* sensitive more than once! As a result, my focus and priorities have often been quite different than many of those who've surrounded me in my daily life—including those in the Church. Most of the time I've felt like I didn't quite measure up when it came to achieving success in its various forms such as career, finances, personal accomplishments, and even the way we typically define success in ministry. While my life has not always displayed many of the typical outward signs of success as defined by western culture, I have long been convinced that God measures success in terms of *faithfulness,* rather than merely by outward circumstances. Faithfulness in our individual lives may, or may not, lead to something that resembles our outward ideas of success—but it *always* leads to success in God's eyes.

With this paradigm in mind, my desire has always been *to be found faithful.* I have struggled with many things in life, but my relationship with Jesus is not one of them. In the words of an old country Christian song (yes, there is such a thing!): *He's the one thing I do right.*

There are many things I wish I did better. There are many areas of habit, discipline, accomplishment, and character where I've often wished I was further along. I wish I was more consistent. I wish I was kinder. I wish I was more patient. I wish I was more disciplined and focused. I wish I always responded in love. I wish I was bolder, more confident, more together. I wish my thoughts toward myself and others always lined up with His. I wish, I wish, I wish ...

But I am where I am. While that doesn't mean I intend to throw in the towel and *stay* where I am—I am absolutely committed to pressing on to lay hold of absolutely everything Jesus created me to be—it *does* mean that regardless of where I currently am (or am not) in the process, there is one thing I *know* beyond any possible shadow of doubt:

God loves and accepts me.

He loves me for who I am. Right here and right now. Because right here, right now—I'm complete *in Him.* Right here, right now—I'm *accepted* by Him. Right here, right now—I'm *wanted* by Him.

So are you.

The desire to be more like Jesus is fabulous! It is our sacred privilege to be conformed to His image. Christ in us is the hope of glory! This is not about spiritual laziness or license to sin. **What it *is* about is knowing His love and acceptance of me is *not* contingent upon how well I have jumped through the latest spiritual hoops.** It is based simply on His nature, His desire, and my union with Him through the finished work of the cross. When I asked the Lord the question about faithfulness, I had an epiphany. When I beat myself up for not being further along in certain areas of life, I'm focusing on what I *don't* do well. However, I felt the Lord was challenging me to focus instead on what I *do* best.

And He's still the one thing I do right.

By that I mean there is no significant strife in my relationship with God. I'm consistently secure. I don't waver in my knowledge of His love. I can honestly say I've fallen more in love with Him year after year—for decades. I know He is always with me, always for me, and always near. I know I can access His presence anytime, anywhere.

Even though He is equally accessible to *all* His children, I know many still question that reality. Considering this, the question about faithfulness became clear. The Lord isn't nearly as concerned as I am about how well I am , or am not, doing in a multitude of areas where I think I need to get my act together. However, what He does desire *is that I will be faithful with what I do know.* What I know best is this:

I know how to get to His heart.

And if *I* can—anyone can. Seriously, if I'm "qualified" to know Him intimately—with all my flaws and all my inglorious messiness—then I know it is possible for absolutely *anyone*. Because the number one thing you need to understand is this:

> *"We cannot love God with all of our heart, until we know He loves us with all of His heart. "*
>
> **–Mike Bickle**

Intimacy with God is *never* based on performance.

Never. Ever. Really! And if you take only one thing away from this study, I pray it will be this one priceless truth.

That's not to say our choices don't matter. They do! Poor choices and wrong actions *do* have consequences—sometimes devastating ones—but that is not the focus of this study. The focus of this study is on the one choice that matters above all others: **The choice to believe.** Therefore, our focus won't be on what we *do*, it will be on what we *believe*. Because what we believe to be true about God, not to mention what we believe about who we are *in* Him and *to* Him, will affect virtually every other area of our lives—especially our pursuit of His heart.

As I began to research what was "out there" on this particular topic, I discovered that most material on the subject of intimacy with God has been written from a fairly linear and intellectual perspective. The focus is often theological, or on what we need to "do" in order to "get" intimacy. Some actually left me chuckling. Can you imagine a sunset translated into a mathematical equation? How about listening to Siri recite

Byron? Ever watched a robot dance a romantic waltz? In each of these examples, there is a huge piece missing:

The heart. *And intimacy with God is all about the heart.*

This study attempts a more devotional approach. While I certainly want it to be informative, my hope is that you will find more than pages and pages of information. Useful information is great, **but my intention is to engage your heart**. More importantly, I believe that is God's desire too.

> *"While our mind is good for crunching numbers, analysis, and arguing about God, it's not so good at knowing the love that goes beyond our mental knowing! Only our heart has the capacity to experience God in a way that defies explanation."*
>
> **-Mel Wild**

Always remember that God is the initiator in this great romance. That's good news! Because what He starts He will finish (Phil. 1:6). As John said, "We love Him because He first loved us" (1 John 4:19). He longs for us to be with Him where He is (John 14:3). He invites us to come boldly to His throne of grace (Heb. 4:16). He invites us to abide in Him and He promises to abide in us (John 15:4). He invites us to come to Him—even in our weariness and imperfections—to find rest (Matt. 11:28). He promises that *nothing* will separate us from His love (Rom. 8:38).

Nothing. Ever. Not here, not in ages to come. Because not *one* of these great and precious promises is based upon our "performance." Not one.

But wait a minute! Doesn't obedience matter? Didn't Jesus say *"If you love Me, keep My commandments"?* (John 14:15).

> *"If God's promise is only for those who obey the law, then faith is not necessary and the promise is pointless."*
>
> **-Romans 4:14 NLT**

Yep, He did. But which commandments did He refer to? How obedient is obedient enough? How many commandments do you have to keep before you can rest confidently in His love?

~The Ten Commandments?

~The 613 laws of Moses?

How good is good enough?

How many commandments do you have to keep to:

~Lean your head on His chest like John did?

~Wash His feet with your tears like Mary did?

~Pour out your heart to Him like David did?

~See His glory like Moses did?

~Be His friend like Abraham was?

The answer is zero. As in zip – zilch – none.

Jesus said the *greatest* commandment was to love Him—and the second was to love others. He said *all* of the law was summarized in these two commandments. **So from Jesus' perspective, it seems like *the main thing* is the commandment to love.** Which, in my mind, makes the most important question this:

How do we learn to love?

I think the answer is incredibly simple:

By being loved.

> ~By running into His arms, right here, right now—**just as you are**.

> ~By climbing up into His lap secure in the knowledge you are wanted *and* accepted—**just as you are.**

> ~By resting in the knowledge that He's not frustrated or disappointed in you. He's not impatiently waiting for you to get your act together. He already saw every fear, every failure, every broken promise, and even every time you'd push Him away, but He still chose you—**just as you are.**

Intimacy with God is *never* based on performance, but to access the love He has so freely given, we *do* need to respond. We need to respond in faith. **We need to *believe*.** We need to believe:

~We love Him *because He first loved us.*

~It is finished! Past, present and future—all our sin is covered. We are beloved and accepted before the throne of grace. Always.

~The veil has been torn. There is a door standing open in heaven—that *no man* can shut.

Through that open door, access has been granted. Now and forever. Period. It doesn't matter what you do or do not feel—it only matters what you believe. Draw near to God and He *will* draw near to you. He's already there waiting. There is *no* separation on His end. None.

Because intimacy with God is *never* based on performance.

Never. Ever. Really! I hope and pray that as you journey into the deeper waters of intimacy with a good and gracious Father who loves you more than you can possibly fathom, you will become thoroughly convinced of this reality. Resting completely secure in the reality of His acceptance is the anchor that allows us to dive ever deeper into the endless ocean of His love … without fear.

Questions for digging deeper:

1. Do you agree with the statement "intimacy with God is never based on performance"? Why or why not?

2. What role do you believe faith plays in drawing closer to God?

3. Have you ever found yourself trying to "earn" God's approval? What would change if you **really believed** you are wholly accepted, cherished, delighted in, and beloved—just as you are?

4. Do you relate to God more easily through your intellect or through your emotions?

5. Have you ever been afraid of letting your emotional guard down before God? If so, why?

6. Close your eyes for just a moment. Focus on a moment when you sensed that God was particularly near. What was it about that moment that stands out?

7. Imagine yourself back in that place of closene
   you've never felt His nearness, imagine what it might
   feel like). From that place, ask the Holy Spirit to reveal
   any lie you believe about how He sees you. If He shows
   you something, ask Him to replace that lie with the
   truth.

8. Seal the moment in prayer. Pray from your own heart or
   use this prayer starter:

Father, thank You for the love and acceptance that are forever mine in Christ. Help me to see myself as You see me—a beloved child in whom You are well pleased. Expose and break the power of any lie that keeps me from the fullness of Your love and restore the beauty and simplicity of daily intimate communion with You. ~In Jesus' name, Amen

Thank you, Abba...
... that you love me.
That we can be so close
& I can lean on you. Lay into
you. Rest in your arms on your
shoulder. You are everything
I've ever needed. And I reading
forward to more of you... more
gold... deeper, closer, stronger.
Thank you Jesus. & You have my
treat my attention. Forgive.

Week 2
The Intimacy of Shared Suffering:
"Love on the Cross"

Suffering. The word likely invokes all kinds of emotions and images—most of them highly undesirable! So why on earth would a topic like suffering be included in a study on intimacy with God?

When we think about the people we are closest to in our lives, we often have the deepest bond with those with whom we've walked through difficult times. Relationships that don't transparently share their suffering and heartache are rarely as deep as those that do. Considering this, it isn't difficult to understand why there is a depth of intimacy in shared suffering that can't be fully developed any other way. As we journey through life on a fallen planet, we *all* suffer at some point (see John 16:33). The question is, will you allow the suffering of this current age to deepen your relationship with the Lord, or drive you from Him?

Before we explore this concept further, I feel it is important to say a few things about what this weeks' topic *isn't* about:

1. It isn't about willingly subjecting ourselves to a myriad of self-imposed sacrifices and needless suffering to somehow prove our piety to God.

2. It isn't about God "allowing"—or even worse *sending*—a bunch of horrible things into our lives to somehow teach us "deep" lessons we couldn't learn any other way.

3. Finally, it isn't about rationalizing sin and failure by justifying and re-branding the consequences of our own foolishness and labeling it as "suffering for the sake of Christ."

Instead, what I do hope to stir within you this week are these two concepts:

1. That Jesus identifies with *our* suffering, and wants us to *willingly* share our heartache with Him to a degree that is often far beyond our comprehension.

2. That to truly *know Him* ultimately means sharing with Him in His own suffering.

Let's dive in!

~Study~

Read Philippians 3:1-16

I love the book of Philippians in general because it is a "real-world" kind of book. It's clear from his writings, that Paul had a brilliant mind and understood deep theological concepts in a way few ever have. Aren't we all glad the Holy Spirit saw fit to allow us to glean from Paul's insights through the pages of Scripture! But I've always seen Philippians as unique among Paul's writing. It is generally understood that Paul wrote Philippians while confined to a Roman prison. That fact makes the overall theme of the book, which could be described as "joy in the midst of suffering," all the more remarkable—and all the more vital for us to understand.

While I love the entire book, it is Philippians 3:1-16 that the Holy Spirit has drawn me to repeatedly. These verses reveal truths that establish a foundation of unshakeable joy and unbroken communion with God, even while living in the midst of a fallen, broken world.

From the exhortation in the first verse to rejoice:

> *Whatever happens, my dear brothers and sisters, rejoice in the Lord. I never get tired of telling you these things, and I do it to safeguard your faith.*
> -Phil. 3:1 NLT

To the challenge to press on to lay hold of *everything* it cost Jesus so much to purchase (verses 12-14), there is a deep compelling within the words to abandon all for the sake of the

One who is all in all. Nowhere is that sense of compelling deeper than in verses 10-11:

> That I may **know** Him and the power of His resurrection, and the fellowship of His sufferings, being conformed to His death, if, by any means, I may attain to the resurrection from the dead.
> -Phil. 3:10-11 NKJV (emphasis mine)

Each time I read the words, *I want to know Him,* it is as if I can literally taste the longing in Paul's heart. I can taste it, because my own heart is filled with the very same longing.

I want to *know* Him.

If you are reading these words, that is probably the cry of your heart, too.

But what does that really mean? What does it mean to *know* Him? Even more specifically, what does it mean to know Him *in the fellowship of His suffering*?

I already mentioned some of what it *doesn't* mean, but to discover a bit about what it *does* mean, let's back up a little further. Earlier in chapter 3 (verses 4-6), Paul provides several details regarding his background. Really, it is a recap of his "spiritual pedigree." If anyone had any reason to feel proud of their spiritual heritage and accomplishments, it was Paul!

Yet despite his many accomplishments, Paul *willingly* laid down all his accomplishments and considered them "rubbish" for the sake of Christ. *But what things were gain to me, these I have counted loss for Christ* (vs.7). Paul wanted to *know* Christ—at absolutely any cost. All of this begs one simple question:

Why?

Now, if you've been in the Church for any period of time, you probably know the correct *theological* answer to that question. Paul gives it to us himself:

> Yet indeed I also count all things loss for the excellence of the knowledge of Christ Jesus my Lord, for whom I have suffered the loss of all things, and count them as rubbish, that I may gain Christ and be found in Him, not having my own righteousness, which is from the law, but that which is through faith in Christ, the righteousness which is from God by faith. -Phil. 3:8-9

> *"We all know people who have been made much meaner and more irritable and more intolerable to live with by suffering: it is not right to say that all suffering perfects. It only perfects one type of person...the one who accepts the call of God in Christ Jesus."*
>
> **-Oswald Chambers**

It is the great exchange—trading our filthy rags for God's righteousness. Certainly, that is a gift worthy of our all! On some level, we all know it's true. Yet a quick look around reveals that while most believers intellectually acknowledge this truth, *precious few live as though they actually believe it.*

But Paul was one who did.

Why did Paul consider Christ worth his all? I suggest it wasn't simply because He was God and Paul wasn't. I suggest it wasn't because Paul knew it was the right doctrinal answer, or even because he knew he should be grateful for all God had done.

Those things certainly are a part of the equation, but on their own they would have never carried Paul through the many things he suffered. The only power strong enough to overcome *any* obstacle is simple:

It's love.

More specifically, it is the love of God. Paul had personally *tasted* the love of God. Really, you could say Paul had learned to be-loved. And because he had "experience(d) the love of Christ, though it is too great to

> *"And I pray that you, being rooted and established in love, may have power, together with all the Lord's holy people, to grasp how wide and long and high and deep is the love of Christ, and to know this love that surpasses knowledge—that you may be filled to the measure of all the fullness of God."*
>
> **-Ephesians 3:17-19**

understand fully" (see Eph.3:19 NLT), Paul wanted to know the One who already *knew him* so intimately and perfectly.

Paul wanted to know the One:

~Who stood beside him and loved him when others abandoned him (see 2 Timothy 4:16-17).

~Who willingly laid down *everything* for him (see Phil 2:5-8).

~Who loved and pursued him, *even while he was still persecuting Jesus and His Church* (see Acts 9:4).

This *isn't* just theology. It also isn't merely gratitude for salvation—as warranted and wonderful as that may be. **This is a *relationship* with a Person that is so deep, so compelling,** *tterly consuming, that nothing short of knowing* *imately—in every way He is knowable—will ever* su.

Even if that means sharing His suffering.

By the time Paul wrote to the Philippians, he had known Jesus for many years—yet he realized there was still so much more of Him to know. Paul's life got turned inside out on that road to Damascus. A true encounter with God will do that to you. An encounter with *Love* will do that to you. Paul wanted to know Jesus—even in His suffering—because he encountered a love that was willing to suffer *for him,* even while he was still merrily persecuting the people of God. When you encounter *that* kind of love, everything else pales in comparison.

When Paul said *"I want to know him"*–he didn't put limits on what he would allow God to reveal of Himself. Most of us do.

> *"Can we trust our lives, our futures, and the lives of those we love to God? Can we trust a God we can't control? Can we trust this God whose take on life and death and suffering and joy is so very different from our own? Yes. Yes, we can. Because we know him. And we know he is good."*
>
> **-Stasi Eldredge**

But Paul knew there was a deep intimacy in shared suffering and he didn't choose his own comfort above a deeper knowledge of God's heart. Paul willingly invited Jesus into his own suffering, and—when you consider the anguish Paul carried in his heart for his Jewish brethren, the way he continually poured himself out for the Church, and the ongoing persecution he suffered—it is clear Paul was also willing fellowship with Christ in His.

Because Paul allowed himself to be-loved, he allowed God to align his heart with His own. And because this great love had so deeply gripped his heart, Paul was willing to give anything and everything to make sure Jesus received "the pure spotless bride" He desired.

Long before Paul's awakening to love, Jesus had other disciples, including the twelve He poured His life into over a period of three years. He shared *every* part of life with them. Yet when it was time for Jesus to suffer—with the exception of John (and several of the women who served Him)—they all fled. I don't

> *"But God demonstrates his own love for us in this: While we were still sinners, Christ died for us."*
>
> **-Romans 5:8**

think it's any coincidence that John, the disciple who often self-identified as *"the disciple Jesus loved,"* is the only one of the twelve who followed Jesus all the way to the cross. John, the one referred to as the "beloved disciple"—John who leaned his head against Jesus' chest—*this* John was among the few privileged to share Jesus' intimate final moments on earth as man.

Was it easy? I'm sure it couldn't have been. But in John's willingness to literally "be there" for Jesus in His suffering, he was an eyewitness to the deepest and most profound demonstration of love the world will ever know.

John was one of the few who "got it" even before the resurrection and the outpouring of the Holy Spirit. Fortunately, we have the benefit of hindsight and know how the story ends. I don't think it is any accident that Philippians 3;10 mentions knowing Jesus in the "power of His resurrection" and *then* in the "fellowship of His suffering. Apart from knowing He *is* the Resurrection and the Life, most of us would never willingly lay down *our lives* for His.

Think of Peter, who was so filled with fear after Jesus was arrested that he denied even knowing Him. Not once, but three times! But once Peter encountered the restorative love of the risen Christ—a love that met him *in his deepest place of failure and regret*—he became unstoppable. This once fearful and impulsive "speak first, think later" disciple came to know the power of love in such a deep and intimate way that, according to tradition, when faced with his own death, he chose to be crucified upside-down not considering himself worthy to be crucified in the same manner as his Lord.

> *"God wants to be loved for Himself, but that is only part. He also wants us to know that when we have Him we have everything."*
>
> **-A.W. Tozer**

Again, the point here isn't martyrdom or subjecting ourselves to sacrifices God isn't asking us to make. The point is, like Paul, *I want to know Him*—at any cost. There are some revelations of His heart and character that cannot be known apart from the intimacy of shared suffering. Jesus was willing to go to any lengths to demonstrate His love. He hung on that cross naked, reviled, and rejected, *yet completely unashamed and undeterred in the depths of His love for us.*

Considering such great love—and considering such great *vulnerability* and *risk*—I want Him to have everything it cost Him so much to purchase. I want Him to have everything He desires from my life. I want to let Him into every area of my heart.

And I want to know *every* part of Him that is knowable.

Questions for digging deeper:

1. Why do you think it is important to let Jesus share *our* suffering before we can truly share *His?* List some Scripture references to support your thoughts.

2. What are some of the ways you can intentionally allow the Lord into your places of greatest pain and loss? Conversely, what are some of the ways you might be keeping Him out of those places?

3. Read Psalm 55:12-14, Isaiah 53:3-12, Luke 13:34, 1 Timothy 2:4, and 2 Timothy 3:12. How do these verses help you understand some of what knowing Him in the fellowship of His suffering" might look like?

4. Read 1 John 4:18. How might this verse apply when it comes to allowing God to share more of His own heart with us?

~Stir~

"For we do not have a high priest who is unable to empathize with our weaknesses, but we have one who has been tempted in every way, just as we are--yet he did not sin."
-Hebrews 4:15

It is amazing to me that God not only knows everything about us, but that He actually *identifies with us* and *sympathizes with us* in our weakness and pain. Many years ago, He revealed this truth to me in a personally profound way.

I had not been walking closely with the Lord for very long when I began serving in a ministry for single moms. It was my first time serving in any kind of leadership capacity, so it isn't difficult to imagine that I was encountering a fair amount of spiritual warfare as I stepped out into this new arena.

One time the "opposition" seemed especially intense. I was helping with a special event and the entire week of the event I felt like I was getting beat up one wall and down the next. I was dealing with the fallout from long-term issues with rejection at that time, and let's just say the things I was experiencing were playing right into those old tapes. I was not feeling particularly loved or affirmed from *any* direction.

As worship began the night of our meeting, I was broken and spent. The worship leader began singing and, in the safety of God's presence, the dam in my heart burst. I poured my heart out to Jesus and found myself complaining to Him that I did not feel loved or supported. As soon as that plaintive cry escaped my lips, I saw a picture of Jesus on the cross and instantly felt incredibly ashamed of my whimpering. After all He did for me for the sake of love—who was I to not *feel* loved? As I contemplated the demonstration of His great love, I was expecting to hear a gentle rebuke for my unbelief and lack of perspective, but instead He said something that absolutely shocked me:

> *"It is the kindness and mercy of the Lord that leads us to repentance."*
>
> **-Romans 5:8**

I know just how you feel, beloved. I didn't feel loved either.

No exhortation to quit whining and get it together. No backlash for my lack of gratitude. No conviction, and certainly no condemnation. Just compassion and comfort. *He knew how I felt.* He *cared* how I felt. Despite His great suffering and sacrifice, He thought *my* suffering—though so ridiculously small in comparison—was important and He wanted me to know it.

I've never forgotten that and never will. That sweet moment of validation and understanding spoke volumes to my hurting heart and had far greater impact than even the very gentlest rebuke could ever have had. He knew my need wasn't to be corrected—my need was to be heard and understood. To Him, my needs weren't small and unimportant; they were valid and very, very important to Him.

Your needs are important too. He wants you to know and believe that. We have a myriad of unhealthy ways available to us to deal with our pain, but when we realize the Lover of our Souls:

~Knows *everything* about us

~Cares about *everything* that concerns us

~Wants to share *every* part of our lives

It really does bring such sweet freedom.

When we allow ourselves to be-loved in our brokenness and pain, we learn one of *the* most powerful spiritual lessons we can ever apprehend: **learning to run *to* Him in our pain and brokenness, rather than away from Him in disappointment, shame, or regret.**

His arms are always open. Always. Remember, intimacy with God is *never* based on performance. Even when you feel like you should "get your act together"—God sees *and* cares about what you're going through.

The astounding flip-side of this equation is that when we become secure in His love and know He is always willing to meet us where we are, our hearts authentically become more and more in tune with His. And when we become more in tune with His heart, we care about what He cares about. While God doesn't necessarily "need" our companionship—He is perfectly complete within Himself—He does *greatly desire it*. He longs for those who will press in to share the areas where His own heart still breaks over the great brokenness in our world. Above all, I believe His heart aches that so many of His beloved children have yet to run into His open arms.

Some time back I had gotten distracted in the morning and did not spend time with the Lord. At some point later in the day, I finally made some time to re-connect with His heart. As I came bounding into my own little "secret place" I cheerily called out, "Here I am Lord, Your wayward child!"

I wasn't expecting a reply, but I got one anyway. One that stopped me dead in my tracks and brought me to my face in gut-wrenching intercession:

> *"All praise to God, the Father of our Lord Jesus Christ. God is our merciful Father and the source of all comfort. He comforts us in all our troubles so that we can comfort others. When they are troubled, we will be able to give them the same comfort God has given us. For the more we suffer for Christ, the more God will shower us with his comfort through Christ."*
>
> **– 2 Corinthians 1:3-5 NLT**

How I wish all my children were so wayward.

It wasn't so much the words. It was *how* He said them. I could hear—and actually *feel*—the pain and longing in His voice. Momentary distractions or not, I was secure in His embrace. But many of the ones He loves so deeply are still far from His heart. For them, He aches.

I could have moved on. I could have brushed that sweet, intimate glimpse into His heart aside and kept things light. But I chose to share the moment with Him. I allowed my heart to be broken by something that breaks His.

Those invitations await us all the time. The God of all Creation has made Himself knowable and vulnerable to us. Jesus, our Immanuel, wants to walk through life with us deeply sharing our most intimate moments. Even more astounding, He wants to invite us to share His own heart—even the places of His greatest longing and heartache.

At the end of the age, each of us will stand before Him. When that time comes, I want to be able to say I've finished *all* the work He's given me to do. I desperately want to hear those precious words: "Well done good and faithful servant." But there is one thing that propels me even more. Beyond failing to finish all my earthly assignments, it would absolutely devastate me to stand before Him on that day and make what I would consider to be an agonizing discovery:

That I could have known Him more.

I *don't* want that to happen. Instead, I want to join Paul in the deepest cry of his heart:

That I may know Him.

I want to know Him in the power of His resurrection (we *need* the power of His resurrection), but I also want to know Him in the fellowship of His suffering.

I want to know Him *every* way He is knowable.

How about you?

Questions for personal pondering:

1. Can you relate to the tenderness of God revealed in the story at the beginning of this section—why or why not?

2. Is it easier or more difficult for you to deeply connect with God:

   -When you've failed (whether real or imagined)?

   -When you're discouraged or disappointed?

   -When you're experiencing sorrow or grief?

3. Do these answers reveal anything new to you about your relationship with the Lord?

4. Most of us, at one time or another, have missed God's invitations to share His heart at a deeper level. Can you think of a time that may have happened in your own life? If so, what can you learn?

~Start~

I hope some of the information in this week's lesson has been helpful and has also engaged your heart. Since these lessons are intended to be interactive between you and the Lord, the following simple suggestions are provided to help enhance your connection with His heart:

Quiet Communion: Find a time when you can have a few moments of quiet. Prepare elements of communion and intentionally set your focus on the cross. You may find it helpful to re-read the gospel accounts of the Last Supper and/or Jesus' trial and death, focusing on whatever parts of the texts the Holy Spirit leads *you* to. With your focus fixed on this most glorious example of sacrificial love, ask the Lord to simply reveal His love personally *to you*, in whatever form that takes. Don't get hung up on what you do or do not feel—just be present and mindful before Him. As you feel ready, partake in the elements of communion in true union with Him.

Intentionally Seek His Heart: Make a commitment over the next week to intentionally set aside time to ask the Lord what's on *His* heart. Don't make it a point of striving—just ask, wait a few moments, and if you don't have any clear sense of what He may be showing you, move on. But keep asking in the days ahead. If you do have a clear sense of what He is sharing with you, ask Him how He wants you to respond. Consider making this a regular part of your personal devotional time if it isn't already.

<u>Crafted prayer:</u> Make a brief list of the things that stood out from this week's lesson. Turn those points (whether they are things you are thankful for, areas where you want to see change, places where you need to be more open to His Spirit, etc.) into a written prayer that specifically expresses your heart and desire. Consider praying this prayer frequently in the days ahead to keep it fresh in your heart.

Week 3

He's in the Waiting:
"Love in the Tomb"

Waiting. Could there possibly be a more despised concept in western culture? In these days of instant gratification and instant access to just about everything, waiting has become a foreign concept. Yet the exhortation to "wait on the Lord" is found throughout Scripture. Anyone who has walked with the Lord for more than about five minutes can testify to the fact that God rarely does things on our timetable!

Some things don't develop quickly. Trust is one of those things—and intimacy requires trust. Like it or not, waiting, in all its various forms, gives us the opportunity to develop, and exercise, trust. It gives us the opportunity to *know* Him better. There are facets of His character hidden for us—just waiting to be discovered—*in* the waiting.

Sometimes waiting looks like long stretches of time where our lives outwardly appear to display the exact opposite of everything God has promised. Other times the wait may be relatively short in the overall scheme of things, but due to the severity of circumstances, every single moment of waiting is an agonizing assault against everything you believe. Times of waiting have the potential to drive us *from* God, or drive us *to* Him—it all depends on how we choose to respond as we wait.

This week, I want to focus on two potential *opportunities* we have in times of waiting:

1. The opportunity to discover Him *in* the waiting.

2. The opportunity to bless Him while we wait.

In our "study" section this week, we'll look at a family that had to wait through some excruciating circumstances, but came through the wait with much more than they ever anticipated!

~Study~

Read John 11:1-44

Who doesn't love the story of Lazarus? It is such an incredible story of hope and life. At least it is when you read it with the benefit of hindsight! But for Martha and Mary—not to mention Lazarus himself—I'm sure there were many moments along the way they would have liked to have skipped.

This is a family who knew Jesus intimately. In fact, Mary of Bethany is the one so frequently seen sitting at His feet.

Martha's personality and gifts were different than those of her sister. Though she was not always as dialed into Jesus' heart as Mary was, Martha was close to Him too—and Jesus loved her deeply. He was a frequent guest in their home. Given their relationship with Jesus, it is certain the entire family knew of His miracles and had no doubt seen many first-hand. However, despite their close relationship with Jesus, they were *not* insulated from personal tragedy.

One day the brother, Lazarus, became extremely ill. The sisters sent word to Jesus saying, "Lord, the one you love is sick." They knew Jesus loved them and they believed He would come to heal Lazarus. Instead, He responded in a way that to our human sensibilities seems a bit shocking.

> *Now Jesus loved Martha and her sister and Lazarus. So when he heard that Lazarus was sick, he stayed where he was two more days.* -John 11:5-6

What? Yep, He stayed right where He was—for two whole days. And while He stayed away, Lazarus died.

It's hard for us to comprehend. He could have come sooner. But He stayed away for a reason that blows me away. He stayed away *because He loved them.*

He waited...

~Not because they did something wrong

~Not because they didn't pray just right or believe just right

~Not because He was mad at them

He waited because He loved them.

Then, after it seemed far too late to do any good at all, Jesus shows up. Although their manner was different, both sisters said exactly the same thing to Jesus when they saw Him. "Lord, if You had been here, my brother would not have died." How often do we say similar things? When things don't go the way *we* think they should, we cry out, "God, where were You, why didn't You come?"

> *"'My thoughts are nothing like your thoughts,' says the LORD. 'And my ways are far beyond anything you could imagine. For just as the heavens are higher than the earth, so my ways are higher than your ways and my thoughts higher than your thoughts.'"*
>
> **-Isaiah 55:8-9 NLT**

Yet sometimes He doesn't come, *because He loves us.* Sometimes He is doing something far greater than what we see on the surface. Sometimes He wants to **reveal Himself** to us in ways that would never be possible apart from waiting.

There are times it may look and feel as though God is indifferent to our needs and unaware of our suffering, but nothing could be further from the truth. In fact, when *we* grieve, so does He. When Jesus went to the grave site with Mary and Martha, He wept right along with them—even though He knew what He was going to do! We often misunderstand His intentions, because we want relief right now. But sometimes He wants to do more than we're able to hope or ask. God never caused Lazarus to become sick, but when it happened, Jesus knew it was an opportunity to reveal more of Himself.

The family in Bethany knew Him as a man of God—but He wanted to reveal Himself as God the Man.

He wanted to reveal His glory.

God *will* come. Faithfulness is an immutable facet of His character. But He doesn't always show up on our timetable. At times He waits precisely *because* He loves us. He comes when it brings Him the greatest glory, and *us* the greatest good. Sometimes that means He'll come after all of our ideas of how He should answer have died and lie rotting in the grave. But the Author of Life is *never* limited, not even by death. Often, the longer He waits, the more staggering, amazing, marvelous and miraculous His ultimate answer will be.

> *"Delayed answers bring answers with increase. Delayed answers bring answers with character."*
>
> **-Bill Johnson**

That was certainly the case in Bethany.

After Lazarus had been in the grave four whole days, Jesus spoke three simple words that turned tragedy into triumph; "Lazarus, come forth." And Lazarus did, grave clothes and all! What was dead, made alive. What was lost, restored. There was no flash, no thunder, no trumpet blast, just three simple words. God spoke, and it was.

He does that in our lives too. Even after we resign ourselves to the loss of our dreams. Even after we begin to settle for less than what we once believed possible, convinced that God has denied our prayers. Then, after it seems far too late, Jesus shows up. He speaks. Suddenly tragedy is turned into triumph, and hope is resurrected—eternally. Because when something has died and then rises again.

It lives forever.

And *that* was the point. Jesus wanted to give them a much greater revelation of Himself. They knew Him as a healer. They knew Him as a friend and a comforter. But He wanted them to know Him at a much deeper level. Really, I think He wanted them to know Him as God. He wanted them to know Him as

> *"Hope that is seen is no hope at all. Who hopes for what they already have? But if we hope for what we do not yet have, we wait for it patiently."*
>
> **-Romans 8:24-25**

the One who has power over the grave. He wanted them to *know* Him—really know Him—as the Resurrection and the Life.

But to know Him as the one who resurrects:

~Hopes that have died

~Dreams that have died

~Purpose that has died

Something needs to actually die.

He can't reveal Himself as the One who does the impossible, unless the situation really is **impossible.**

~Not difficult

~Not challenging

~Not unlikely

39

But completely, unequivocally, undeniably—*impossible.*

There are so many stories throughout Scripture that bear witness to this truth. Abraham was 75 when God promised him a son. He was the ripe-old age of a 100 when Isaac was born. Talk about impossible! Abraham tried to take things into his own hands at one point when God didn't seem to be moving fast enough (can you say "Ishmael"?), but Abraham's very human solution was *not* God's plan and God still did what *He* promised—in His timing.

How about David? Against all odds, David was anointed as Israel's next king when he was a very young man. It must have seemed surreal. But it certainly wasn't an easy or quick path to the throne, especially when David was forced to live a life on the run from his jealous, demented predecessor, Saul. At one point David even pretended he was mad—behaving more like a crazed wild-animal than a king—to avoid danger (see 1 Samuel 21:12-14). Yet David *still* became king, just as God said.

Then there was Joseph. He was a teenager when God gave him dreams of greatness. Yet life wasn't looking so great for Joseph when he was sold into slavery by his own brothers. To make matters worse, he was then falsely accused by his master's wife and unceremoniously tossed in prison to rot, all because he acted *righteously.*

But God was with Joseph—even in prison. And many years later, *in a single day,* Joseph was elevated into a prominent position of authority, second only to Pharaoh himself, in the most powerful nation in the world.

There is a point in each of these stories. They waited. And waited. And then waited some more.

But God did what He said.

He was faithful to His promises. In fact, He was faithful *even when they didn't wait perfectly.* He was faithful because that's who He is. And because it's who He is, He'll be faithful to you too.

> *"Take courage my heart*
> *Stay steadfast my soul*
> *He's in the waiting*
> *Hold onto your hope*
> *As your triumph unfolds*
> *He's never failing"*
>
> **-Kristene Dimarco**
> (from the song, *Take Courage*)

~Do things seem impossible right now?

~Does it look as though God has forgotten you?

~Are some of your dreams dead and buried and stinking up the tomb?

Good. Because the One who "waits because He loves you," knows *exactly* what it's like to inhabit a tomb. But Love also has this sneaky habit of finding a way when there is no way. Love can never stay buried. Just ask the early disciples. They thought all was lost. At least they did on Friday.

But then Sunday came.

Sunday is coming for you too. In the meantime, know this:

He's in the waiting.

Questions for digging deeper:

1. Read Psalm 27:14, Psalm 130:5-6, Galatians 5:5, James 1:2-4. What do these verses teach you about waiting on the Lord?

2. Read John 11: 21-27 and John 11:32-35. Why do you think Jesus responded differently to Martha and Mary although they said basically the same thing? What do they teach you about His compassion and individual knowledge of us?

3. Read Isaiah 40:31 in several different versions (if possible, look at the NKJV, the NIV, and the NLT). What do you notice about the different ways the verse is translated? From these different translations, what additional things can you learn about God's purposes for us "in the waiting"?

4. John 11:14-15, and John 11:40 provide powerful keys to the story of Lazarus. With these verses in mind, can you think of an instance from your own life where God didn't show up in your timing, but the ultimate outcome ended up being much more fruitful and glorious than it would have been if God had merely done what was originally asked?

~Stir~

"Those who wait for the Lord will gain new strength; they will mount up with wings like eagles, they will run and not get tired, they will walk and not grow faint."
-Isaiah 40:31 NASB

It's funny how a particular passage of Scripture can speak to you deeply through the years, but then one day you hear it as if you've never heard it before. You see it like you've never seen it before.

You understand it like you've never understood it before.

This happened to me recently with the story of Lazarus. I've long cherished the hope contained in this story. God has spoken to me deeply through many different parts of the story, at many different points in life. I've even written about it and taught on it—starting years ago.

But reading it again recently took my breath away. Not only did it fill me, once again, with abounding hope, but it also filled me with something else:

Gratitude.

> *And let us not grow weary of doing good, for in due season we will reap, if we do not give up.*
>
> **-Galatians 6:9**

It filled me with gratitude for the *privilege* of waiting.

Jesus could have kept Lazarus from dying, but He *didn't*. It certainly isn't because He wasn't invited into the situation–He absolutely was. He heard the cries of Mary and Martha and He fully intended to answer—*just not when and how they thought He would*. He planned to answer in a different and more astounding way. It was a timing issue. We've probably all heard teaching along these lines. Maybe we even believe it.

But for me, this was different. I didn't just "see" it this time. I *knew* it at a whole new level. I knew it at a whole new level, because, well, I've known waiting at a whole new level.

I've seen an awful lot of hopes and dreams crash and burn in my lifetime–particularly over the last decade. It seems there have been so many that not only do I not have time to recount them, I don't have the *heart* recount them. It has been such a long and ongoing process, that I finally got to the point where I pretty much gave up on *ever* resuscitating many of my lost dreams. I buried Lazarus and moved on.

Well, that was the plan anyway. It worked for a moment or two.

It worked until my heart was stirred again with reality of resurrection life. It worked until I understood–*really understood* **that to experience resurrection, you need to first experience death.**

If you want to understand that *all* things are possible with God, you need to actually be faced with the impossible. If something is just sick (or broken, or rearranged, or shelved, or delayed, or whatever) it could ... possibly ... potentially ... conceivably ... get better naturally.

But when something is *dead*, well, when something is dead, there is nothing–that's right *nothing*–you can do.

You can't try a little harder. You can't come up with a list of steps to success. You can't make your own reality. You can't say or pray just the right words. You can't conjure up just the right amount of faith that will obligate God to move.

You can't *do* anything.

But He *can*.

And *that* is the point. The point is that sometimes–because He loves us–He waits. He waits so we can believe.

Really believe.

"Did I not tell you that if you believe, you will see the glory of God?" (John 11:40).

He did tell me that. And I'm beginning to see His glory *even in*

> *Biblically, waiting is not just something we have to do until we get what we want. Waiting is part of the process of becoming what God wants us to be.*
>
> **-John Ortberg**

45

the waiting. It's been a long process. I wouldn't have chosen this path, but I also don't regret it.

Some years ago, I served with a large global missions organization. Twice a year we would have candidates for field service come into our office for training. As part of their training the candidates learned to publicly give their testimony. One day in chapel, I was listening to the testimony of a remarkable young woman. She was recounting the amazing things God had done in her life in a very short period of time. Many of those blessings were the very same things I had been praying about for many years without any sign of breakthrough or movement. I was so excited for her—God used those things to reveal more of Himself to her and she was literally glowing with joy and gratitude—but I also had a familiar ache in my own heart where those desires remained unfulfilled.

> *"My soul waits for the Lord More than the watchmen for the morning; Indeed, more than the watchmen for the morning."*
>
> **-Psalm 130:6 NASB**

I told the Lord I was so happy for her, but I longed for a similar testimony of breakthrough in my own life. Jesus told me I *did* have a testimony: *I had a testimony of perseverance.*

I *still* have a testimony of perseverance—and at this point it is a much longer one! Thankfully, I have seen breakthrough, and even a few miracles, in a couple of those long sought after situations. But for the most part, I am still waiting. The temptation is to believe I have done something wrong and that is why I haven't seen the answer. I choose instead *to believe Him.*

I choose to believe I will *see* the glory of God.

Not only will I see Him in the answer, I will see Him in ways I never could have if He answered when I first started asking. In fact, I already have. That has been the greatest beauty and blessing of the waiting, *knowing Him in ways I would not have otherwise known Him.* In the waiting I've come to know Him as:

> ~The bridegroom who faithfully and patiently waits for His bride, and as the Father who enduringly aches for His children to come home.

> ~The One who is infinitely patient and kind *with me.*

> ~As Immanuel, the One who daily takes my hand and walks with me regardless of what the day may hold.

> ~As the One who meets me in my weakness and Whose grace is completely and wholly sufficient in *every* season.

And this is just the tip of the iceberg. Someone once told me if you learn to blossom in the desert, you can blossom anywhere. That is what waiting has taught me. Waiting has taught me that absolutely *everything* I need is found in Him.

I wouldn't trade that for anything.

Jesus said, "Blessed are those who have not seen and yet have believed" (John 20:29). There is a special blessing reserved for those who choose to persevere in faith though they've not yet seen the answers to their prayers. Faith always pleases God, but enduring faith blesses Him more than we can fathom. What a priceless privilege it is to know that when we wait in a place of trust and faith, it moves His heart so deeply!

Although I eagerly await the day His promises will come to pass (and they will), far more compelling than seeing the reality of God's promises fulfilled, is the promise of seeing *Him*. I believe one of the most profound verses in all of Scripture on the concept of endurance is a very simple one: *"He* (Moses) *endured as seeing him who is invisible"* (Heb. 11:27). As amazing as the promises are, the promises are not the reward—*Jesus is the reward.* And He is *in* the waiting with us, longing to be discovered in new and wonderful ways.

The tomb will open. Hope will rise. Faith will become sight. And when the promise is fulfilled, God will reveal Himself to be more than you ever could have hoped or imagined.

But He's just as glorious here and now—*in* the waiting.

Questions for personal pondering:

1. Think of some of the areas where you've been waiting for God to move. Take some time and list some of the ways you've experienced God's faithfulness *in* the waiting.

2. Read Hebrews 10:35-36. What do these verses reveal to you about the link between confidence and endurance?

3. Think of a situation in your life where it has been particularly difficult to wait. Ask the Lord who He wants to reveal Himself to be in these specific circumstances.

~Start~

I hope some of the information in this week's lesson has been helpful and has also engaged your heart. Since these lessons are intended to be interactive between you and the Lord, the following simple suggestions are provided to help enhance your connection with His heart:

What if? While we are waiting, there are often areas where our hearts become worried or anxious. Typically, these worries are brought about by imagining a "what if?" outcome that excludes God's faithfulness. Take a piece of paper and divide it into two vertical columns. On one side identify some of your "what if's"—the worst-case scenarios that may be consciously or subconsciously disturbing your peace. Ask the Lord to reveal the specific scriptural promises that counter your fears. List those on the opposite side of the paper. Meditate on these promises and speak them over yourself regularly. Ask the Lord to hide them in your heart and make them real to you. In the days ahead, each time you find yourself drifting into to a place of worry or fear, remind yourself of His specific promises.

Who are you to me? In question #3, you asked the Lord who He specifically wanted to reveal Himself to be in your most difficult place of waiting. During your time with the Lord over the next week (or for as long as you feel led), ask the Lord to expand on how that facet of His character specifically applies in your current situation. It will be helpful to search the Bible for specific instances where He revealed that attribute of His character. I find it helpful to journal my thoughts as I often receive revelation as I write (as opposed to "hearing" something and then recording it).

Crafted prayer: To end the week, once again make a brief list of the things that stood out from this week's lesson. Turn those points (whether they are things you are thankful for, areas where you want to see change, places where you need to be more open to His Spirit, etc.) into a written prayer that specifically expresses your heart and desire. Consider praying this prayer frequently in the days ahead to keep it fresh in your heart.

Week 4

Shared Triumph:
"Love that Never Fails"

Triumph! Now we're getting somewhere. Who doesn't love the big triumphant finish? Everyone loves a winner. Everyone loves the big victory. Everyone loves to *see* the answer to their prayers—especially when the answer has been a long time in coming. Long awaited victories are defining moments for all of us.

However, just as there are blessings in times of waiting and sorrow, there are both blessings and challenges in times of victory. Every season of life presents its own unique opportunities to either lean into, or away from, God's heart. Times of triumph are no exception.

Here are two of the opportunities related to "shared triumph" that I want to explore this week:

1. The more intimately we come to know Jesus, the more deeply we learn to access the victory He has already won on our behalf.

2. Each personal victory in our own lives provides the opportunity to build history with God and, as a result, bring us to a place of deepened trust.

Before, we jump into our "study" section this week, I want to take a moment to focus on the triumph of all triumphs—Jesus' victory on Calvary. His victory *is* our victory. Talk about shared triumph! In fact, the whole point was that it would be shared. He took on our defeat, so we could experience His triumph.

Over the past couple of weeks, we've looked at opportunities to lean into God's heart during times of both suffering and waiting. Whenever we suffer or wait, if press into His heart, there is always a place of redemption. But when Jesus calls us to take up our cross and follow Him— or when He asks us to watch and wait with Him—we *don't* do these things in an attempt to *obtain* victory. Rather, we are drawn to share every part of life with Him *because of a victory that has already been won.* The key to learning to live in a place of trust, abundance, and abiding rest is found in laying hold of this most amazing of all realities.

If Jesus made a way for us to enter the Holy of Holies—if He made a way for us to enter into deep and unbroken communion with Himself—if He defeated death itself—*is anything beyond His reach?* Of course not. This is why becoming deeply rooted in the finished work of the cross is the very thing that positions us to appropriate His victory into ever expanding spheres in our own lives, in the lives of those around us, and even into the world itself.

In our "study" section this week we'll look at a couple different examples of shared triumph from the Scriptures. Through these stories, we'll observe how the early Church's understanding of Christ's victory on Calvary, along with the history they had personally developed with Him, made them *unstoppable* as carriers of His love!

~Study~

Read Acts 12:1-16 and 16:16-34

The first story we'll look at this week is the story of Peter's miraculous release from prison in Acts chapter 12. At this point in history, many things had happened since Jesus' resurrection and ascension. The early disciples experienced the outpouring of the Holy Spirit on Pentecost, and then, a while later, in a miraculous series of events no one could have predicted, there was a huge paradigm shift when the Holy Spirit was poured out on the gentiles—making it abundantly clear God's plan of salvation was for *all* who would believe.

However along with these great blessings, came an increase in persecution. At the beginning of chapter 12, James (the brother of John) had already been put to death by Herod when Peter is seized. But the night before Peter was to be brought to trial, in vs. 5 we're told: "...the church was earnestly praying to God for him."

They had already lost James, and it wasn't looking too good for Peter.

~But the church was praying

~The church was waiting

~The church was believing

~Because they knew *whom* they believed

The time since Jesus' ascension must have been a whirlwind. There were huge losses, but there were also amazing victories. *Each one of those victories became markers that kept the early church focused on who He was, rather than on the current trials.*

And He is a miracle working God.

Remember Paul's prayer in Philippians 3? (See Week 2.) Paul wanted to know Christ in the fellowship of His suffering *and* in the power of His resurrection. Just as knowing Jesus in His suffering *is* part of knowing Him here on earth, knowing Him as the victorious Lord of Hosts, *before* we have experienced the full expression of His victory, is also an integral part of knowing His heart. One does not contradict or eliminate the other, both are expressions of His nature. There is a one huge difference though:

> *"Every loss is temporary. Every victory is eternal."*
>
> **-Bill Johnson**

The losses and suffering are temporary, but every victory is eternal.

While His compassionate nature will never change, our need for comfort and compassion most certainly will. When the fullness of His kingdom comes, every single tear will be wiped from our eyes once and for all. Not only that, He will finally have His long awaited pure, spotless Bride. What an amazing day that will be! In the light of His presence all of our questions, pain, and past suffering will melt away forever, but the glory of His victory—*and every victory we've apprehended in Him*—will be ours to share with Him forever!

Peter was about to apprehend a bit more of that victory:

> *The night before Herod was to bring him to trial, Peter was sleeping between two soldiers, bound with two chains, and sentries stood guard at the entrance. Suddenly an angel of the Lord appeared and a light shone in the cell. He struck Peter on the side and woke him up. "Quick, get up!" he said, and the chains fell off Peter's wrists. -Acts 12:6-7*

I love that picture! Instead of being offended that trials kept coming, Peter became more confident in the midst of them. In fact, he was so confident, he was able to take a little snooze right in the middle of the ordeal!

If you recall, this wasn't Peter's first rodeo. He was imprisoned before (Acts 5) and miraculously freed by an angel. It would seem Peter allow that experience to become one of those "markers" in his history with God.

But that doesn't mean Peter knew exactly *how* God was going to come through. After all, they had just lost James. Despite that tragedy, things were about to get a little humorous. The church is filled with faith and praying fervently. Peter is filled with peace and resting while imprisoned. Basically, they're doing exactly what they should be doing. Then the miracle happens—*and they don't even realize it!*

Peter thinks he's having a vision. When he finally "comes to himself" he goes to the prayer meeting in process *for him* but they don't believe it's really him! They think it's his "angel!"

This is all so human and relatable. **Yet still so filled with faith**. Their faith was demonstrated in how they positioned their lives before the Lord—*not* in how they felt, or even in how quickly they caught on to what God was doing.

This story is encouraging to me! It's reassuring because I don't always catch on so quickly either. But even when I don't, *God is still at work.* When I have significant challenges before me, I purpose to set my face like a flint to focus on Him. **But sometimes I'm so busy staying focused, I'm not able to see the miracles beginning to unfold all around me.**

I'm willing to bet there are miracles unfolding all around you too, but sometimes we need a little divine nudge to push us outside of our limited perspective so we can see them. That's what Peter and those praying for him needed. They stayed focused and in a place of peace because they knew "Whom they had believed" (see 2 Tim. 1:12). But even though they positioned themselves in faith, it still took a moment or two for them to catch up to the reality of what God had already done. Believing God doesn't mean we have a clue about all the details, or that our feelings will be on track with what He is doing, it just means we believe *Him* and we *know* He is faithful.

Paul is another one who understood this. In Acts 16, during Paul's second missionary journey, he and Silas were arrested in

Philippi then beaten with rods—*not* a pleasant experience. But "around midnight" they start singing and having a praise party.

> *Around midnight Paul and Silas were praying and singing hymns to God, and the other prisoners were listening. Suddenly, there was a massive earthquake, and the prison was shaken to its foundations. All the doors immediately flew open and the chains of every prisoner fell off!* -Acts 16:25-26

During the darkest hour of the night, while in chains with their backs beaten and battered, they're singing praise. Essentially, they were thanking Him for the victory, *while they were still in the heat of the fire.* The powerful weapons of praise, thanksgiving, and peace, wielded *before* they saw the victory, broke their own chains *and* everyone else's. Their willingness to trust in a certain, though as yet unseen, victory created an atmosphere of miracles that freed every prisoner and saved an entire family.

> *Nevertheless, I am not ashamed, for I know whom I have believed and am persuaded that He is able to keep what I have committed to Him until that Day.*
>
> **-2 Timothy 1:12 NKJV**

It all goes back to intimately knowing Him. It is being so convinced of who He is that we *know* He is able to keep what we have entrusted to Him, *regardless of our current circumstances.*

Just as there is joy in sorrow and suffering, there is still suffering in the midst of our victories. But which will we magnify? What is our perspective? Let's choose to focus on the victory that has already been won. Let's focus on Love's greatest triumph. I may fail but His love *never* does. He has already proved His faithfulness. His victory *is* our victory. Start praising Him now and those chains *will* fall!

Questions for digging deeper:

1. Read Acts 5:17-32. What impact do you think this incident had on how Peter responded during the events of Acts 12?

2. Re-read Acts 12:12-16. What do you see in this part of the story? Does it encourage you in any way? Have you ever had the experience of praying for something and not realizing the answer was right in front of you? Why do you think we are sometimes slow to see the answer?

3. Read 2 Chronicles 20:1-24. Contrast this with the story of Paul and Silas in Acts 16. What similarities do you see? What differences? What do these stories tell you about the power of praise in difficult, or even impossible, circumstances?

4. Read Philippians 3: 7-11. Does reading this text again in the context of Acts 16 give you any additional insight into Paul's relationship with Jesus? Share your thoughts.

~Stir~

"But thanks be to God! He gives us the victory through our Lord Jesus Christ."
-1 Corinthians 15:57

God often uses unexpected things to reveal areas of our hearts that haven't yet been transformed by His love. This lesson was one of those things for me. I had a much more difficult time writing it than I did with any of the others. When I pressed into the Lord to figure out why, I discovered a surprising answer:

I was believing the lie that I knew more about suffering and waiting than I knew about victory.

It wasn't that I haven't experienced His victory. I have. Many times, and in many ways. But, as I indicated in the previous lesson, there are many key areas where I'm still waiting. There are important things that I'm still *believing* for even as I write this. And frankly, some of those things seem pretty dang urgent.

I thought I was doing a pretty good job keeping my eyes on Jesus and keeping my heart focused on what He *has* done, as opposed to what He *hasn't.* While I *have* purposed to set my mind and heart "on things above" (see Colossians 3:1-2), there was still a place in my heart where I was allowing that little lie to put a damper on my joy. I was allowing it to become a weight I didn't need to carry.

> "*Faith engages the person and promises of God and rests upon them with perfect assurance.*"
>
> **-A.W. Tozer**

I didn't need to carry it because He already did. He carried it all the way to Calvary. I *do* know His victory. His victory *is* my victory. His victory is just as real and just as complete regardless of whether I've seen it manifest in my circumstances or not. The fact that I still believe—that I believe *more* than I did when I first started praying—*is* in itself evidence of His victory.

It's evidence of a victory in my heart.

Remember the story in Luke 5 where a paralyzed man's friends lowered him through a roof to get him to Jesus? When Jesus sees him, He lets the man know his sins are forgiven. Of course, the religious folks blow a gasket at the gall of Jesus to "presume" to forgive someone's sins, so Jesus asks this penetrating question:

> *"Why do you think this way in your hearts? Which is easier to say, 'Your sins are forgiven,' or, 'Get up and walk'?* -Luke 5:22-23

His inference was that healing the man's body was the easier part. But what the man needed *most* was the work only Jesus could do in his heart.

Of course, Jesus ended up healing his body too:

> *"So that you may know the Son of Man has the right and the power on earth to forgive sins," He said to the man who could not move his body, "I say to you, get up. Take your bed and go to your home." At once the sick man got up in front of them. He took his bed and went to his home thanking God.* -Luke 5:24-25

> *"Now faith is confidence in what we hope for and assurance about what we do not see."*
>
> **-Hebrews 11:1**

Beloved one, His victory is your victory too—where you've seen it manifested, *and* where you haven't. He's already done *all* the heavy lifting. He's already defeated the power of sin and death. We are fighting *from* victory—never for it—because **it is already finished**.

I'm so grateful He exposed the lie I was believing so I can more fully embrace His victory here and now. This isn't faith in faith or denying the reality of the challenges I face, just as it is never that for you. It is a matter of focus. It is remembering and *putting our weight on* the greater reality of a victory that has already been won.

Just as we all have circumstantial areas where Jesus' victory has not manifested outwardly, we all also have inward places that His love has not penetrated. God never exposes our weakness to:

~ chastise us

~or shame us

~or even to "discipline" us

He exposes our weaknesses so we can see clearly and walk in greater freedom. It is always truth that sets us free. Each time truth sets us free, we walk in a greater measure of victory

At the beginning of the lesson, I mentioned that one of the main takeaways from this week's lesson is that each personal victory in our own lives positions us to build history with God that bring us to a place of deepened trust. Having developed my own history with God, I find it much faster and easier to return to peace and freedom when the facts of my circumstances contradict the truth of God's word. I know His faithfulness because I've *experienced* it for myself.

There are multiple references throughout Scripture given to Israel as an exhortation to remember. Remember His promises. Remember His deliverance. Remember His faithfulness. Sometimes they did, but often they dis not. Regardless of what *they* did, *I* want to remember. I want to focus on His victory and *remember* the many amazing and miraculous ways He has come through for me. Some have been huge markers in my life, others have been small quiet kisses of His grace. I've learned to ask Him for "rocks of remembrance" (see Joshua 4:1-7) when He has done something really significant in my life—whether it is a breakthrough in my circumstances or in my heart. He is always faithful to answer.

The very first time I had a huge breakthrough many years ago, the Lord helped me mark it by changing the spelling of my name. The whole story is quite remarkable but would take too much space to tell it here. In a nutshell, in a single moment, He delivered me from over twenty years of seeing myself as a victim. Through the story of the paralytic at the Pools of Bethesda in John chapter 5, Jesus helped me lay hold of the fact that no matter how long something has been broken, victory *can* be apprehended in an instant. It was such an incredible marker for me. It was the day I realized my past would never again define my future.

I knew He had done something miraculous and instinctively knew I needed a marker to remember it by, so I prayed that He would give me one. He did.

> *"The greatest miracles of Elijah and Elisha took place when they were alone with God."*
>
> **-Streams in the Desert, February 27th**

About a week before this encounter, I had randomly shared with a friend that when I was around twelve I changed the spelling of my name. I had already experienced a lot of trauma in my life and I think I was trying to run away from who I was. When I talked to that same friend after my big breakthrough, she started crying over parts of my story. I said, "It's okay, I'm *not* that sad scared little girl anymore!" Without her knowing anything about my prayer for a "rock of remembrance," she suddenly blurted out, "You're not Cindi with an 'i' any more, you're Cindy with a 'y'!

As soon as she said it, I felt the inner witness of the Spirit. That was my marker. Cindi with an 'i' tried to run from her pain, but Cindy with a 'y' had been a pretty spunky little girl before life beat the joy out of her. In returning to the original spelling of my name, I was making an ongoing declaration that I was returning to God's original plan for my life.

In *His* plan, I was always a victor, and *never* a victim.

My name change may have been the first huge victory in my life, but there have been others since. However, some of them have happened so quietly, I've needed to stay alert to notice them! I've needed to make sure I stay connected to the reality of His victory even in areas where I haven't yet experienced it. In His presence and in His timing every loss *will* be restored. But are we willing to trust Him *now?* Because, beloved one, *that* is what He's after.

I believe in signs and wonders. I believe we should do the works Jesus did and even greater things, because that's what *He* said (see John 14:12). As we draw nearer to Him, and become more like Him, I believe we will see more and more of His power and glory manifested on a regular basis.

Yet I believe the *biggest* miracle is the transformation of the human heart.

> *"Because of the joy awaiting him, he endured the cross, disregarding its shame. Now he is seated in the place of honor beside God's throne."* -Hebrews 12:2 NLT

His victory *is* our victory. It's already sealed. It's already done. But will each of us allow Him to have the victory *He* most desires as the reward of His suffering:

Our fully conquered hearts.

Questions for personal pondering:

1. Take a moment to think back on some of the greatest ways God has demonstrated His faithfulness to you in the past. How does "remembering" these things affect your faith today?

2. Is your tendency to focus more on what God has done or on what He hasn't done? Do you believe that purposing to focus more on what He has done plays a role in positioning us for future victories? Why or why not?

3. Have you ever believed the lie that your past will limit your future? If so, what did you do to get free (or what *can* you do)?

~Start~

I hope some of the information in this week's lesson has been helpful and has also engaged your heart. Since these lessons are intended to be interactive between you and the Lord, the following simple suggestions are provided to help enhance your connection with His heart:

Rocks of Remembrance   In Question #1 above, you took the time to remember many of your personal stories of God's faithfulness. If you didn't do it at the time, write those victories down. Beside each one, ask for a "rock of remembrance." In other words, ask the Lord for something concrete that will help you to more regularly bring these victories to mind. You may already have stones of remembrance for some of these victories, but for others, you may need to wait on the Lord. Don't make it difficult. If nothing comes to mind today, purpose to ask again at another time. It can be anything – a scripture that you write down where you'll see it, a literal rock with a word and a date (I have several of these!), a picture that has significant meaning, or even something as simple as a specific note in your journal. There are no rules. Be creative. The idea is simply to remember!

Victorious Speech: Our words matter. Ask the Holy Spirit to begin to prompt you when your speech indicates defeat instead of victory. Ask Him to reveal any lies you may believe that keep you from resting more fully in His victory. Seek Him for Scriptures that declare the truth and confess those specific Scriptures each time your thought veer toward familiar lies.

Crafted prayer: To end the week, once again we'll create a crafted prayer. But this week, make your prayer a specific declaration of victory. List the some of the specific things where *you* are seeking God for victory, and craft a prayer that speaks the victorious truth of Scripture over that request. For example, if you are praying for someone's salvation, you could say "Lord thank you for your victory in Joe's life! Thank you Lord that Your plans for Joe. are for good and not for evil, to give him hope and a future. Thank You that You are not willing that any should perish and you have already made the way for Joe's salvation...." If it is for healing, "Thank You, Lord, that by Your stripes I have been healed. Thank You that the blood You shed on Calvary speaks a better word than any doctor's report...." You get the idea. No matter what you are waiting for, heaven has already secured the victory!

Week 5

Divine Partnership:
"Love in Action"

Action. The dictionary defines action as: *the fact or process of doing something, typically to achieve an aim; a thing done, an act.* We've talked a lot over the past few weeks about pressing into the heart of God and really getting to *know* Him in every season of life. We've looked at the intimate opportunity of sharing His suffering. We've looked at finding Him hidden in the waiting. And, last week, we talked about building our testimony and history with Him as we share in His triumph. However, once we are secure in who *He* is, and who we are *to* Him, *we also need to find out what we were created to do.*

So often, we put the cart before and rush into all kinds of service *before* we're secure in who we are. But if we work ourselves into a frenzy without ever knowing—really knowing—that our worth to God has *nothing* to do with our achievements, we will never experience the "unforced rhythms of grace" (see Matthew 11:28 from The Message) that flow effortlessly when we serve out of security and rest. Remember the big take-away from week one? **Intimacy with God is *never* based on performance!** Until we get that, even our very best efforts are likely to be tainted with a mixture of motives.

> *"Jesus gave them this answer: 'Very truly I tell you, the Son can do nothing by himself; he can do only what he sees his Father doing, because whatever the Father does the Son also does.'"*
>
> **-John 5:19**

Jesus had a mission to fulfill on this planet. So do we. Jesus Himself commissioned us before His ascension. There is a reason God doesn't save us and then whisk us all off to heaven. Before Jesus went to the cross, He said He had completed the work the Father gave Him to do (see John 17:4). Like Jesus, our mission is to individually complete the work the Father has given *us* to do. Ephesians 2:10 (NLT) says: *"For we are God's masterpiece. He has created us anew in Christ Jesus, so we can do the good things he planned for us long ago."* Jesus was exceptionally focused on His specific mission and that's our mandate too. We are each accountable for the specific work God has *personally and uniquely* entrusted to us. Like Jesus, we should only do what we see the Father doing.

But we can't do what we see the Father doing, until we can *see* the Father.

That takes intimate relationship.

And that is what we've spent the last several weeks exploring in a deeper way. Once we *are* secure in His embrace, we can clearly hear His heart for the world around us. We become intimate partners with Him in seeing the coming of His Kingdom. Our love grows feet and springs into action.

Because love looks like something.

As we explore the idea of "love in action" this week, I want to focus on these main points:

1. When intimate connection with God is your priority, your motive for "action" will come from a place of love and relationship, and not obligation or a false sense of identity.
2. True love in action means moving as one *with* Him—in divine partnership—in His way and in His timing.

That doesn't mean we shouldn't begin to serve Him until we're sure we've got it all figured out. If that were the case, none of us would ever do anything! As we've discussed in every other lesson, our journey with Him is just that—a journey. Trial and error along the way is part of

> *"So that's where pursuing love begins: gaze at God in his love. Dive into the greatest commandment before getting consumed in the second. In the long run, because of the actions it will produce, this is the most loving thing we can do."*
>
> **-Jon Bloom**

the process of growing and maturing in love. But the whole point is that we *do* mature. Once again, that happens primarily in the context of ongoing relationship.

In our "study" section this week, we're going to take another look at Mary and Martha. Specifically, we'll be looking at a profound turning point in Martha's maturing process.

~Study~

Read Luke 10:38-42

Sometimes I think Martha gets a bad rap. She loved Jesus and wanted to serve Him—just like so many of us. But, also like many of us, *she allowed the service itself to block her view of the One she desired to serve.*

Basically, she allowed herself to get distracted and got her priorities messed up:

> *But Martha was distracted by the big dinner she was preparing. She came to Jesus and said, "Lord, doesn't it seem unfair to you that my sister just sits here while I do all the work? Tell her to come and help me." -Luke 10:40 NLT*

She got her priorities messed up, because she wasn't yet secure in His love. Her cry of "doesn't it seem unfair!" is pretty much the rallying cry of every orphaned spirit.

~It's not fair that this happened to me!

~It's not fair that you helped my sister (or brother) but not me!

~It's not fair that I must do all this work by myself!

~It's not fair that I don't experience Your presence the way others do!

Does any of this sound familiar? I think at one time or another we've all compared our "lot" to that of someone else and, in the process, managed to convince ourselves we were stuck with the short end of the stick. Since Martha didn't know who she was herself, she was not *at all* happy about allowing

> *"True discipleship is about the inner transformation of the soul. Without this transformation, we risk driving people away from God because we will project Him to them through our own wounds, fears, and insecurities, judging their weaknesses according to our strengths. We will hurt them thinking we're serving God. And then we will disciple others to be just like us!"*
>
> **-Mel Wild**

Mary the freedom to be who *she* was. When we don't realize who *we* are, we not only miss the unique beauty and blessings of own calling, but we risk becoming even more distracted when we're jealous of someone else's calling.

That was the *real* problem. It wasn't that Martha was serving instead of sitting with Jesus—it was the attitude of her heart. She was wired to serve in practical ways. That's a good thing. Mary was more contemplative and was wired to serve Him in very different ways. That is also a good thing.

What's *not* a good thing is when we try to impose our calling and predisposition upon someone else.

Martha wasn't secure in who *she* was, so she judged Mary through her own broken lens. Yet Jesus is always reaching out to us and drawing us closer. I love how He addresses Martha:

"Martha, Martha…" (Luke 10:4). The endearing tone of His very gentle rebuke is so comforting. The NLT translates it this way: "My dear Martha." Even though Jesus was correcting her, His tone was one of love and grace. He wanted to draw Martha's attention to the real issue, and, as a result, draw her heart much closer to His own.

Then there is Mary. Scripture says, "Mary chose the better part." As the NLT says, she *discovered* it. That is such profound language. You can choose something as an act of your will, but as we allow our relationship with the Lord to develop and unfold, we *discover* the better part. And the better part is this:

Being with Him. Hearing His heart. Figuring out exactly who you are created to be and being *that* with all your heart.

Once you discover your unique place in His presence and in His purposes, you won't be jealous of the role others are called to play. You will never begrudge anyone else their unique place, because you are so completely satisfied with your own portion. Best of all, when you discover the "better part"—*it cannot be taken from you.*

> "Anyone who knows who God made them to be will never try to be someone else."
>
> **-Bill Johnson**

Mary and Martha both had a place in Jesus' presence, in His affections, and in His kingdom. Mary was secure in her place, Although Martha didn't yet have that security, I think she was teachable. I think she eventually got it. The last reference of Martha in the Bible is in John 12. This is the chapter where her sister Mary anoints Jesus with costly perfume in an extravagant act of worship that Jesus said would always be remembered. But we don't see Martha comparing herself to Mary in this story. We don't see her barging in and interrupting. We don't see her annoyed or frazzled. We don't see her challenging her sister's act of worship. Instead two little words tell us what Martha did. Two little words immortalize her ongoing love for Jesus:

"Martha served." -John 12:2

What a testimony! We're all in process. Wanting to serve God is a *good* thing. It means we've managed to find our way out of the consumerism Christianity that plagues so much of the western church. As I mentioned at the beginning of the lesson, if we wait until we think we have it all figured out, we might never do much of anything. We all learn and grow along the way.

But when you find yourself repeatedly stretched too thin, or burned out, or "worried and upset over all the details"— chances are you've forgotten "*there is only one thing worth being concerned about.*"

That "one thing" is sustained intimate connection with the One we were created to know.

That's why being in His presence is so key. The Great Commission is just that: a *co*-mission. It is a partnership with heaven. That means we need to remain close enough to hear His heart. In Isaiah 6 we see an example of this. Isaiah 6:1 says, "It was the year King Uzziah died that **I saw the Lord**" (emphasis mine). In the space of a few verses (vs 1-8), Isaiah realizes who God is, realizes who he is *apart* from God, and realizes who God has created and commissioned him to be *in partnership with Him*. While in the Lord's presence, Isaiah *overheard* the cry of God's heart. Because he'd already been prepared, from that place of intimate communion, Isaiah was sent out.

When we spend time with the Lord, we grow in our knowledge of who He is and who we are to Him. Once that happens, we begin to hear the things that are *always* on His heart. When we say yes to *His* purposes, we discern our unique role in His plans more clearly.

"Here am I, send me!" is always the response of those who regularly spend time His presence. Love and relationship will always be stronger motivators than religious obligation. There is a place for *all* of us to serve. The harvest *is* plentiful. But the passage about the harvest in Luke 10:2 (and Matthew 9:37) says that we should pray and ask the Lord to *send* laborers into the harvest field.

~Not just those who *want* to go

~Not just those who are *willing* to go

~But those who are *sent*

Even when we're willing, timing is key. God knows what we need, He knows the pieces that need to be in place. He knows the level of confidence and trust that need to be instilled in us before we can be effective for the long haul. He knows the capacity that must be built into us to steward our specific calling. If we jump into service without establishing and maintaining the intimate connection with Him that is necessary to *know* we're being sent, it's kind of like unloading a barrel of buckshot. If you aim broadly enough, you just might hit something. You just might do some good.

But it will never be *the best.*

It's a different story when we're *sent.* Being specifically sent from the presence of God is like an arrow shot from His heart. It *always* hits the target.

Waiting to be sent is sometimes difficult. Good things are often cleverly disguised distractions that the enemy uses to keep us from the best. As I noted at the beginning of this lesson, we value action and achievement. When you have the will and desire to "do something" for

> *"He made my mouth like a sharpened sword, in the shadow of his hand he hid me; he made me into a polished arrow and concealed me in his quiver."*
>
> **-Isaiah 49:2**

God—especially when you've gotten a glimpse of what that something is—it *is* hard not to barrel ahead without Him. However, moving ahead of His presence and becoming distracted from the "one thing worth being concerned about" is *never* worth the cost.

Moses knew something about this. If God didn't go, he didn't go. Period. Moses *knew* his assignment was to take the children of Israel out of Egypt and into the Promised Land, *but he was not willing to fulfill that assignment at the expense of his intimate connection with God.* When God grew weary of the ongoing unbelief of the Israelites, He told Moses to take them into the Land without Him (Exodus 33:3). But Moses said:

> *"If you don't personally go with us, don't make us leave this place. How will anyone know that you look favorably on me—on me and on your people— if you don't go with us? For your presence among us*

*sets your people and me apart from all other people
on the earth."* - Exodus 33:15-16 NLT

Did you catch that? *It's His presence that sets us apart.* It's being a people who only do what we see Him doing. It's being a people who co-labor with Him. It's being a people who live and move and have their being in Him. Mary got this. Martha struggled, but I think she got it in the end. How about you?

Questions for digging deeper:

1. Re-read Luke 10:38-42. Do you relate more to Mary or to Martha? Why? What do you learn about the heart of God toward both Mary *and* Martha from this passage?

2. Read James 2:14-24. With the scriptures referenced throughout our "study" section in mind, how do you reconcile this passage in James, with the other verses we've discussed? (Note: There isn't a right or wrong answer here—this is intended as food for thought!)

3. Read Galatians 3:3-6. Do you see a connection between these verses and the theme of our lesson? If so, what connection do you see?

4. Read John 12:1-8. Contrast the actions/responses of Martha, Mary, and Judas in this passage. What does this story tell you about each of their hearts and their motivations for service? Look specifically at verses 7-8. What message do you think Jesus intended to convey with His remarks?

~Stir~

"I am the vine; you are the branches. If you remain in me and
I in you, you will bear much fruit; apart from me
you can do nothing."
-John 15:5

As in each of the previous lessons, the message in this chapter is personal to me. I have often remarked that I am a Mary in a Martha world. While there are a lot of wonderful things about that, it has also led to a lot of misunderstanding—especially in my own heart.

Although the Lord has taught me time and again to choose the better part—and that is exactly what my heart most longs to do—at times I have allowed the lies of the enemy and the opinions of man (both real and perceived) to diminish my highest and most priceless joy: That of simply being His

We all have our own path in relationship with Him. I am an inside-out person. Although many struggle getting the truth from their heads to their hearts, I have always been the opposite. I sensed certain things deeply in my heart but had no language or theological grid for what my heart knew intuitively. Because I also never heard confirming teaching by respected teachers and mentors, I was convinced I was "doing it wrong."

> *"Revelation has always been the child of relationship more than it is the fruit of intense study."*
>
> **–Kris Vallotton**

In my formative years in the Church, most of the messages I heard were to "do, do, do!" But my heart longed to simply *be* with Him. Initially, this conflict of priorities caused me much confusion. Although I desperately desired to love and serve Jesus with my whole life, I constantly carried a burden that I wasn't *doing* enough. Since I was more interested in spending time with Him than I was in participating in every possible ministry opportunity, I was sure I must be horribly lazy or selfish—or both. But God Himself revealed a different opinion in the matter.

This all came to head after a significant period of transition. At the Lord's invitation, I moved away from my home church and several ministries that were a huge part of my life. The season I moved into was much quieter. At first, I found fulfillment in various prayer ministries, but after a while He had me lay those down too. It was confusing and even frustrating at times, but I knew I needed to trust and follow.

During this same period, my times in the "secret place" with Jesus took on a new dimension. With more frequency and intensity than ever before, I was drawn into a place of deep and intimate communion with Him. I was often so overwhelmed by His presence that I couldn't even speak, let alone pray. Over and over again, I was completely lost in love and worship.

I was so blessed by these times and so wooed by his Spirit that I didn't do much to resist. Although I cherished each moment, deep in my heart I was uneasy. I felt guilty. I thought I was spending way too much time getting "blessed" and not nearly enough time praying for others. Even when I had no other visible ministry, I always knew I could pray. Since there were so many needs to consider, was I wasting my prayer time selfishly pursuing my own fulfillment?

God's response came by way of a familiar passage in the Gospel of Matthew:

> *While Jesus was in Bethany in the home of a man known as Simon the Leper, a woman came to him with an alabaster jar of very expensive perfume, which she poured on his head as he was reclining at the table. When the disciples saw this, they were indignant. "Why this waste?" they asked. "This perfume could have been sold at a high price and*

giving to the poor." Aware of this, Jesus said to them, "Why are you bothering this woman? She has done a beautiful thing to me. The poor you will always have with you, but you will not always have me." – Matt.26:6-13 NIV

The words, "Why this waste?" pierced my heart like a knife. That had been *my* attitude. I thought my time would have been better spent in what I considered to be more noble service to others. Instantly, I realized I *was* being selfish, but not in the way I had thought. It wasn't the needs of others I wasn't considering—*it was the heart of God I wasn't considering.* I was so focused on how being with Him blessed *me*, it rarely occurred to me how much it blessed *Him*. I was so anxious to be of "use" to Him that I almost missed the highest call of all. In simply loving Him, being with Him, and responding to his presence in worship, I *was* serving Him—in the very purest sense.

> *"I take joy in doing your will, my God, for your instructions are written on my heart."*
>
> **-Psalm 40:8 NLT**

You may wonder why I'm sharing this particular story in the lesson that is *finally* about action. Am I suggesting we should all go hang out in a prayer room 24/7 and forget the poor? Should we forget the Great Commission? Not at all!

First, the message here is the same as Jesus' message to Peter (in John 21:22), "You follow me!" Do what He is leading *you* to do. Be who He has created *you* to be. Second, I share this story because this particular season taught me *more* about service and divine partnership than any other season in my life.

It taught me:

~That friendship and fellowship will *always* mean more to Him than a thousand accomplishments.

~That partnership is always dance—a dance He leads—I cannot, and *will not,* go where He doesn't lead, no matter how noble my intentions.

~I don't want my prayers or my service to be "buckshot." I want them to be the arrow sent from His heart. That takes ongoing intimacy.

~As we choose the better part, our lives *will* bear fruit—the exact fruit He desires in each season.

I do have an assignment on this earth. So do you. Love does look like something. First and foremost, it looks like:

~Knowing Him

~Knowing who you are *to* Him and *in* Him

Then–from that secure place of identity—from that place of allowing yourself to "be-loved"—*love looks like making Him known.*

Love looks like making Him known for who He truly is by releasing an authentic representation of His love *through your life.*

When each of us finally fulfill our unique role in doing *that....*

The whole world will "be-loved."

Questions for personal pondering:

1. Have you ever experienced "burn-out" in serving others? How did you respond? What did you learn through that season?

2. Read John 15:1-5. How could you apply this passage could apply to this lesson?

3. Do you believe you've ever stepped out ahead of the Lord in your zeal to serve? Contrast this with what it is like to be sent. You can draw on personal experience, observation, or what you believe the difference might be.

~Start~

We've reached our final week! Once again, I hope some of the information in this week's lesson—and in this entire study—has been helpful and has also engaged your heart. Since these lessons are intended to be interactive between you and the Lord, the following simple suggestions are provided to help enhance your connection with His heart:

> Scripture Reflection: Take some time to quiet your heart before the Lord and ask Him to highlight a key Scripture (or passage of Scripture) from this series. Commit to memorizing the verse, or verses (if you haven't already) and purpose to meditate on that verse, or verses, in the weeks and months ahead. Let it be a "rock of remembrance" (see lesson four) to seal what God did in your heart through this study.

> Dancing with Him: I love the analogy of dancing with Jesus. It is such a beautiful picture of intimate partnership. And yes, guys can dance with Him too! Close your eyes and imagine yourself dancing with Jesus (if the dance analogy doesn't work for you, substitute something that represents intimate partnership to *you*). In that place of moving with Him, ask Him to share what has blessed *Him* as you've sought Him over the past few weeks.

> Crafted prayer: To end the study, we'll create a final crafted prayer. Instead of just making a brief

list of the things that stood out from this week's lesson, make a list of things you want to remember from the study in general. Turn those points (whether they are things you are thankful for, areas where you want to see change, places where you need to be more open to His Spirit, etc.) into a written prayer that specifically expresses your heart and desire. Consider praying this prayer frequently in the days ahead to keep it fresh in your heart.

Above all, always, remember *you* are beloved.

CONTACT INFORMATION

To contact the author, email:
simplefaith247@gmail.com

or visit her website at:
www.cindypowell.org

Made in the USA
San Bernardino, CA
30 September 2017